I0469406

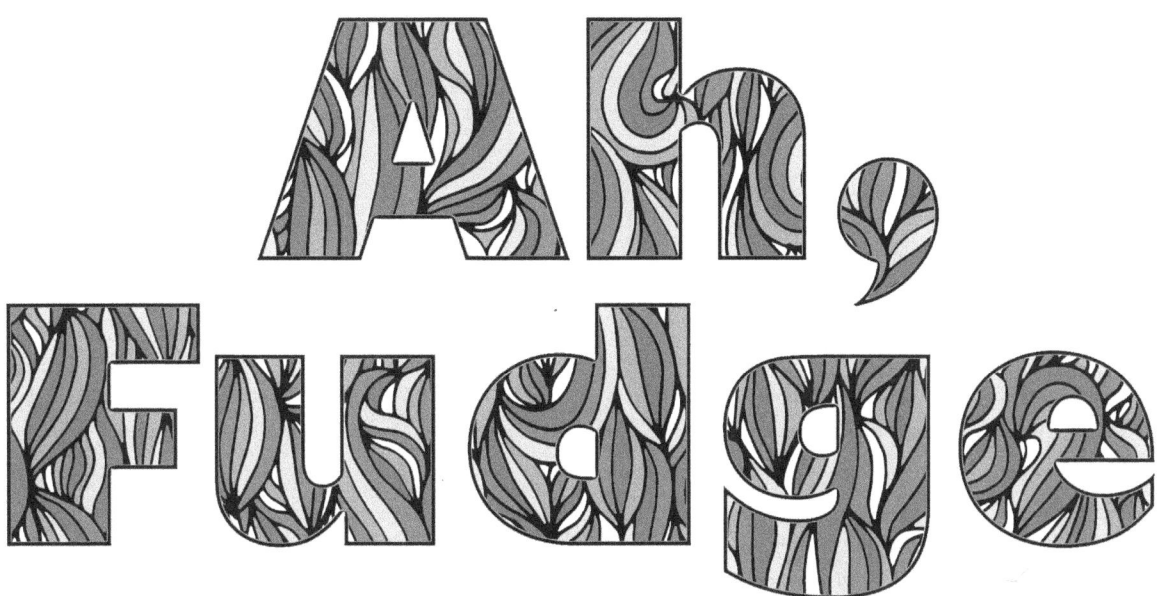

Ah, Fudge

A Very Un-Sweary Coloring Book
for When You're Feeling Like a Pile of
Shiitake Mushrooms

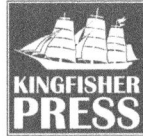

KINGFISHER
PRESS

Special thanks to all the contributing illustrators! © IrinaKrivoruchko © Catherine Glazkova © ziiinvn © makar © oksanka007 © DiviVector © Olesia Agudova © LittleCuckoo © Snezh © totallyPic.com © Smika © Nipatsara Bureepia © Afishka © Helen Lane © passengerz © Hulinska Yevheniia © OlichO © Yudina Anna. Type design: Jake Flaherty

Printed by: Createspace.com

10 9 8 7 6 5 4 3 2 1

Kingfisher Press LLC
Online: www.kingfisherpressbooks.com
Twitter: @KingfisherBksNY
Facebook: www.facebook.com/kingfisherpressbooks

March, 2016
New York, New York, USA

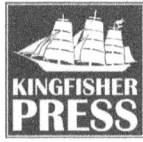

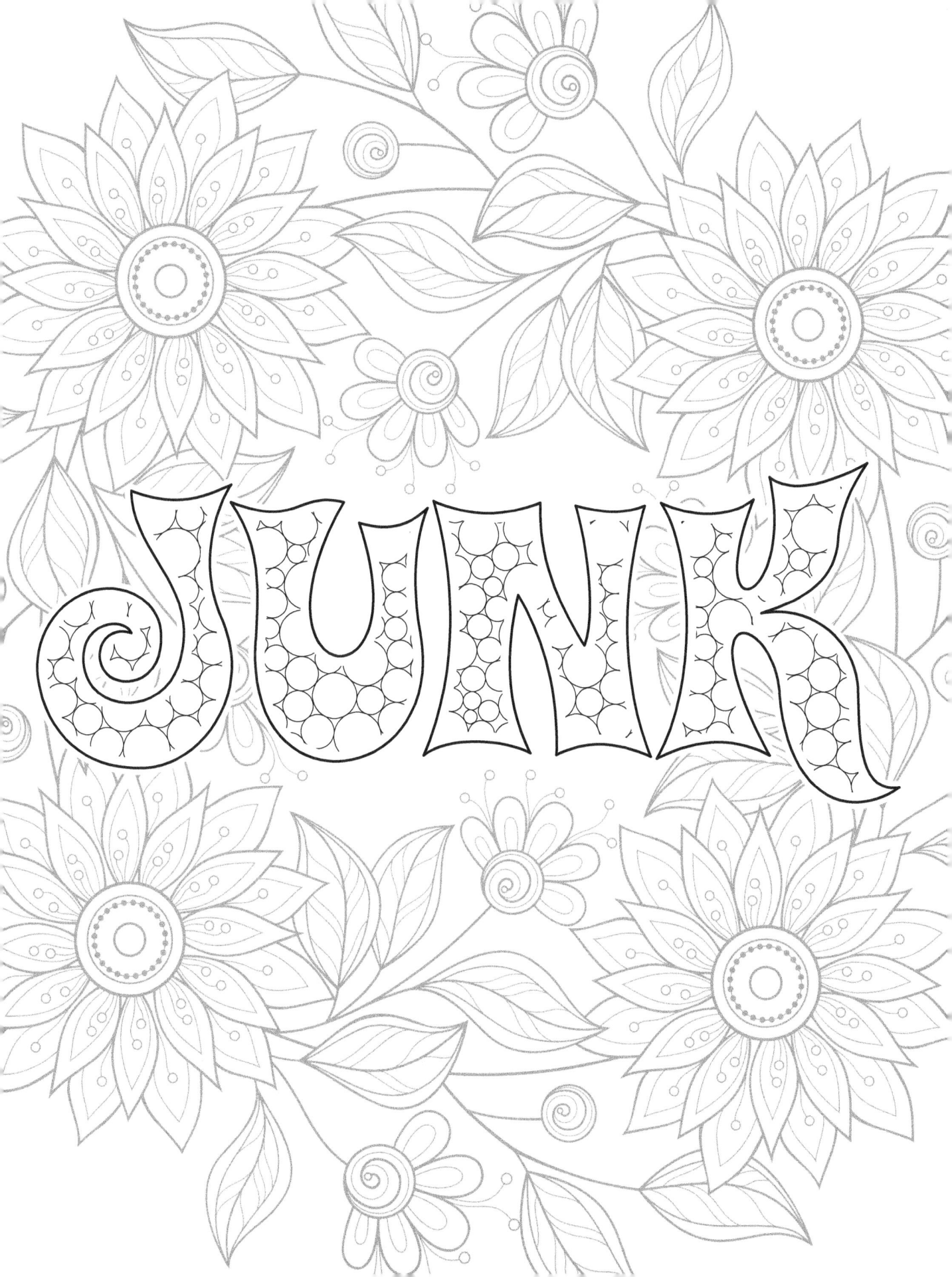

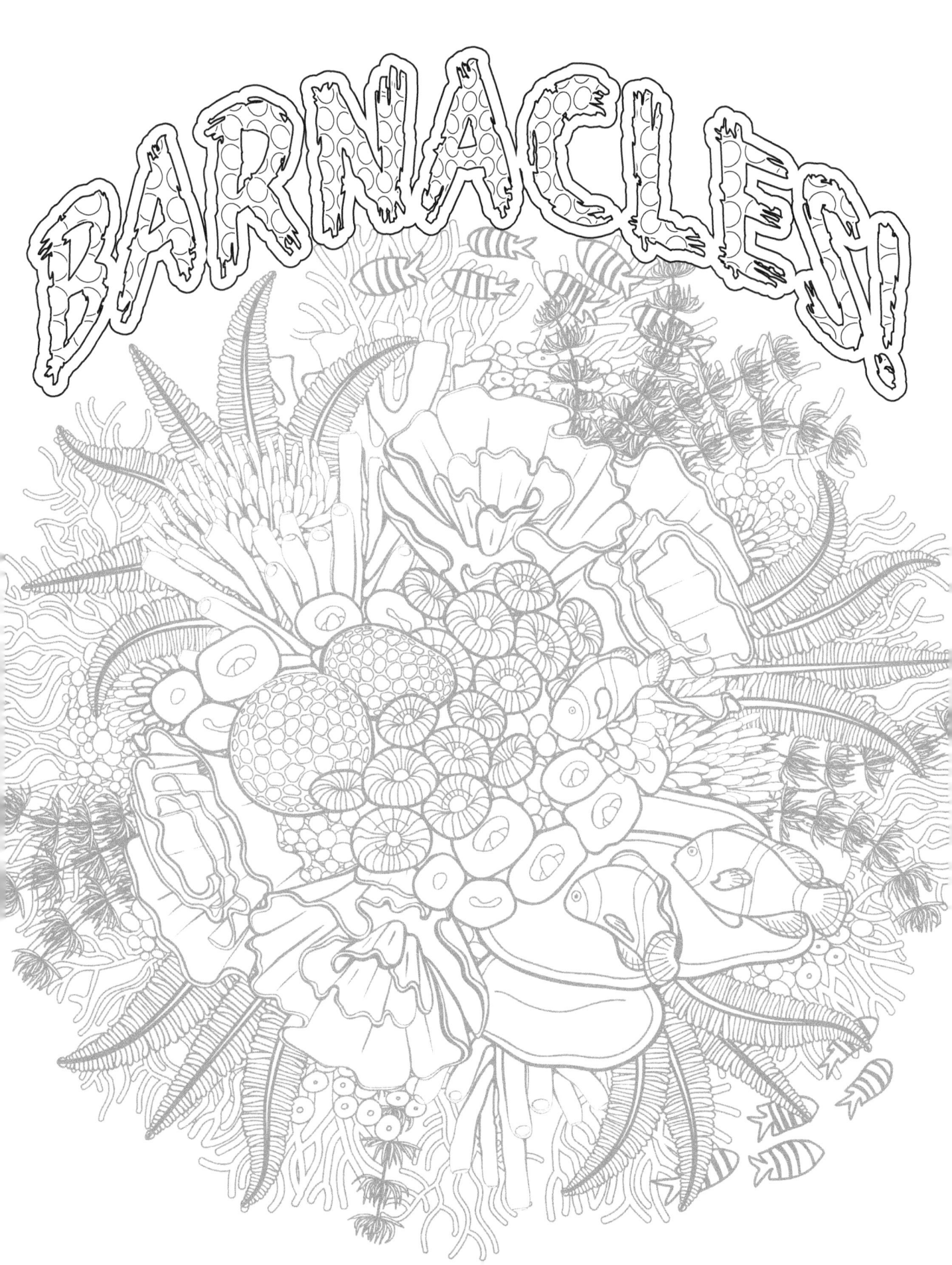

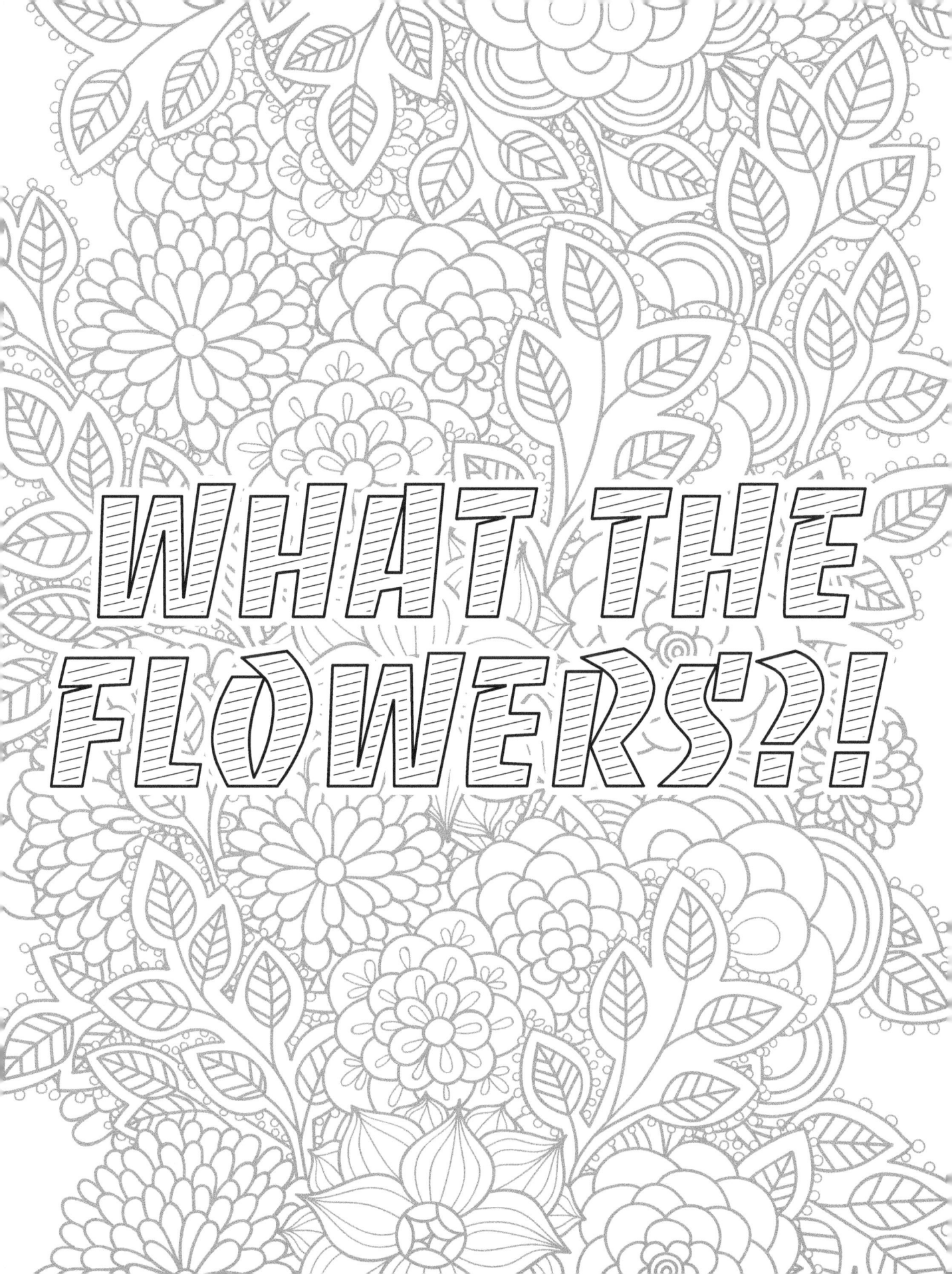

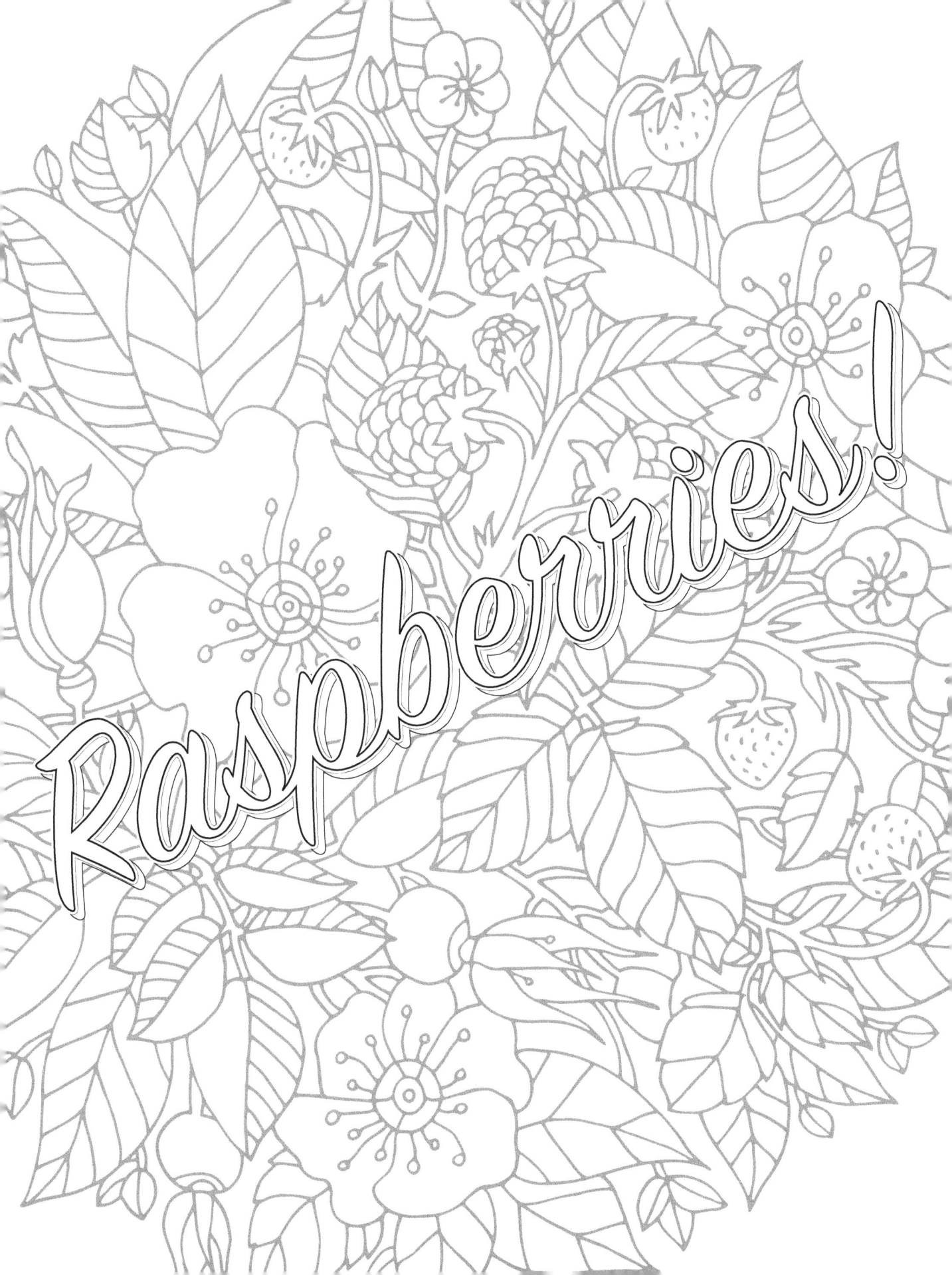

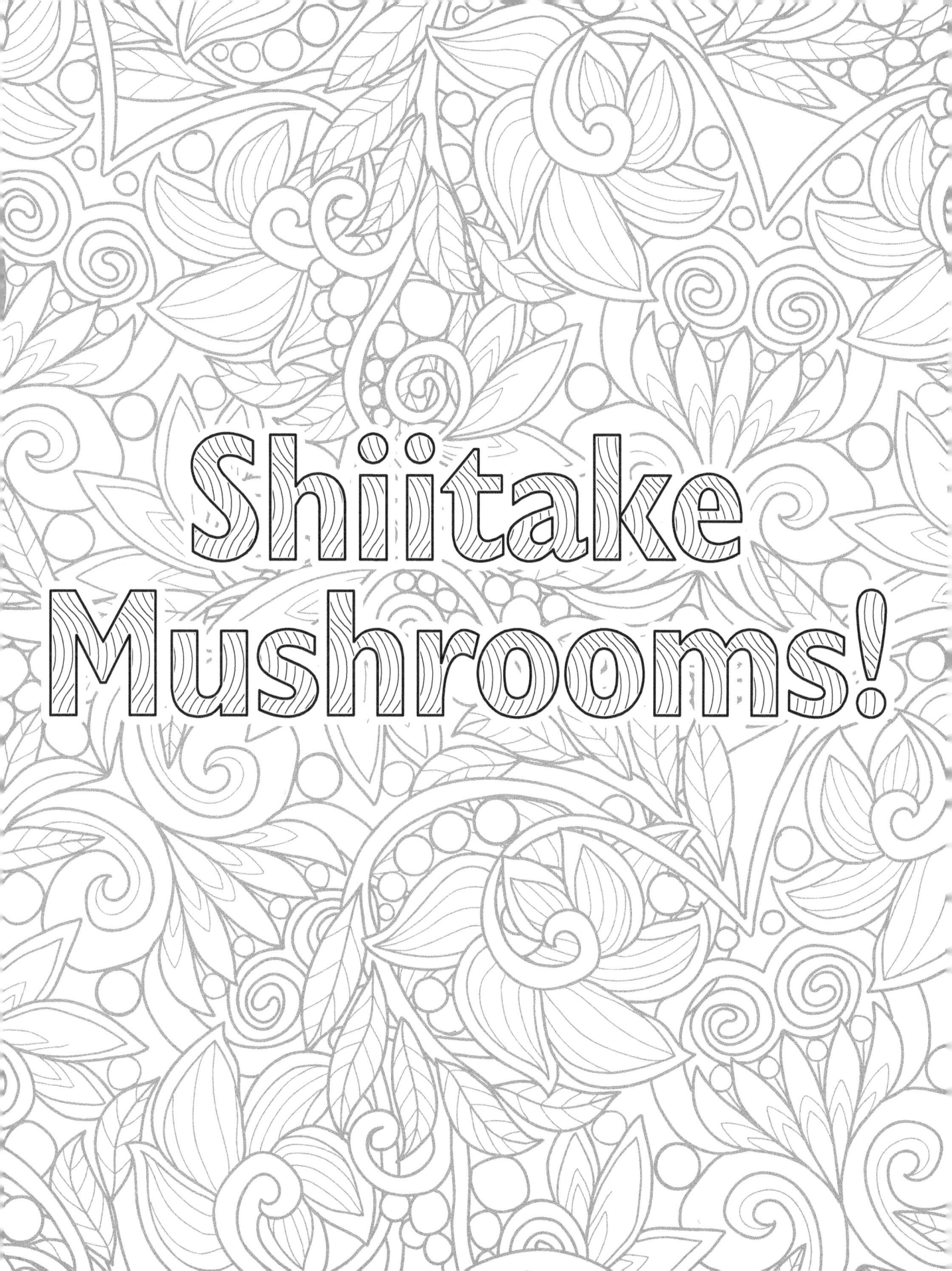

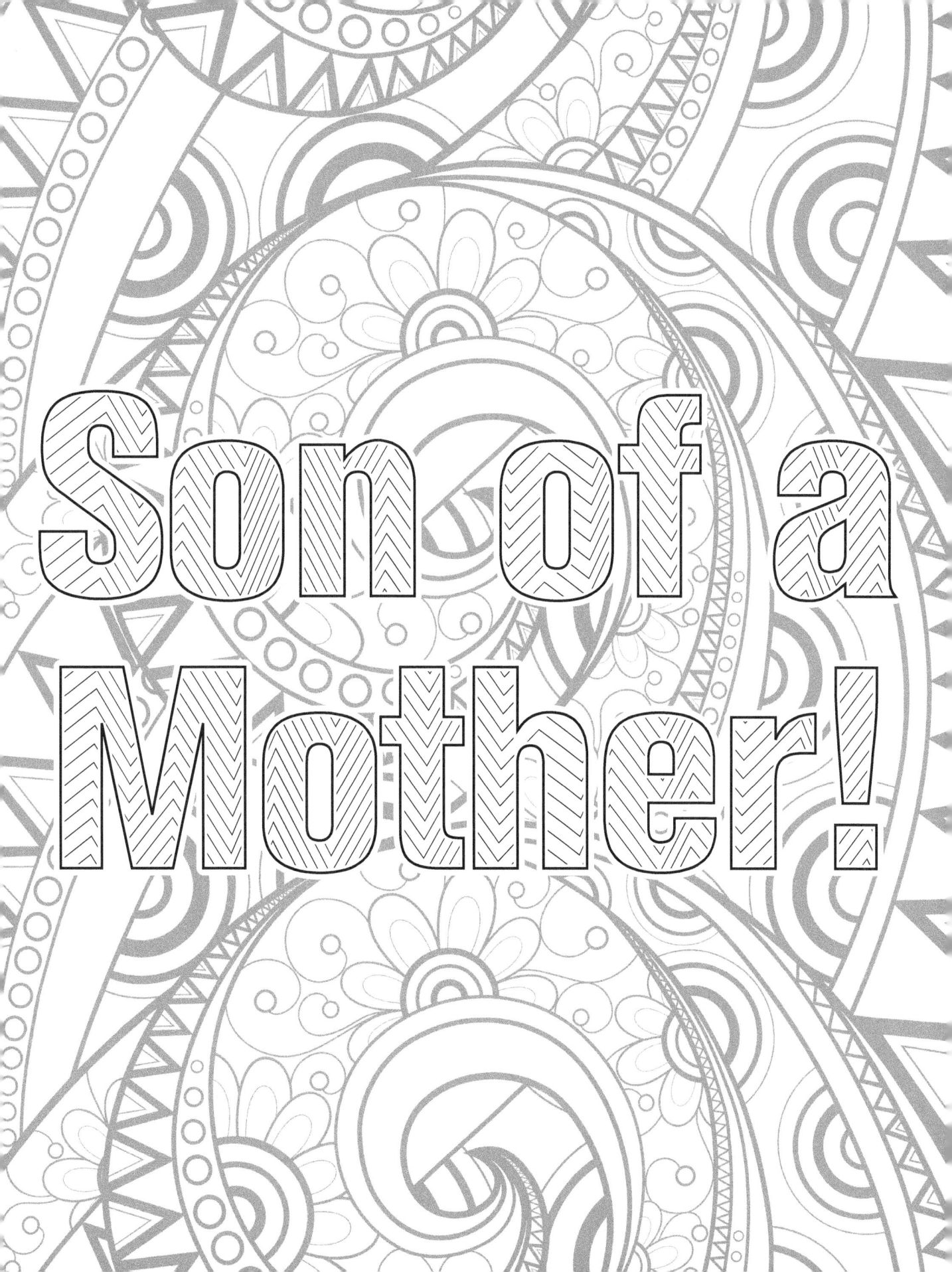

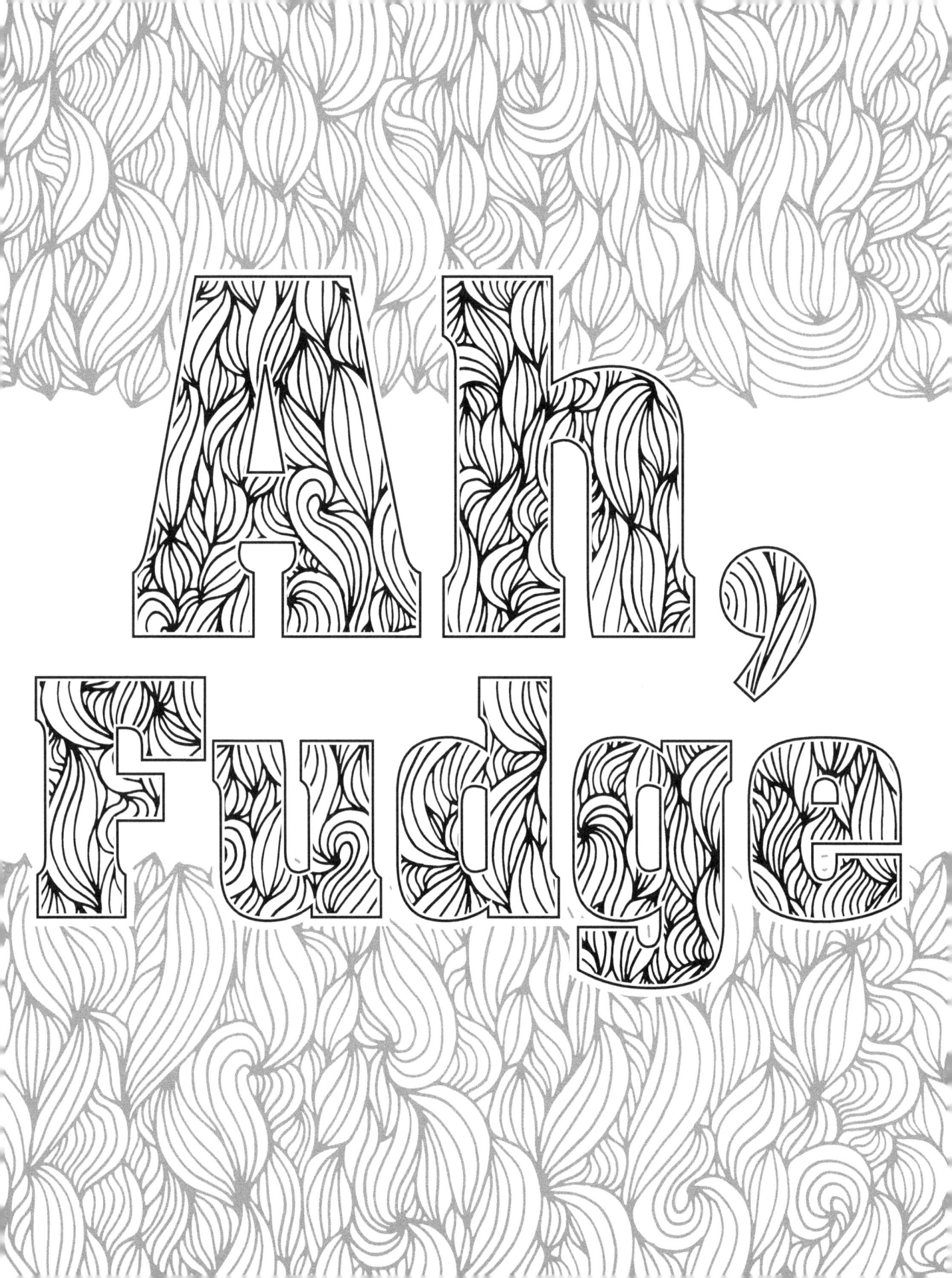

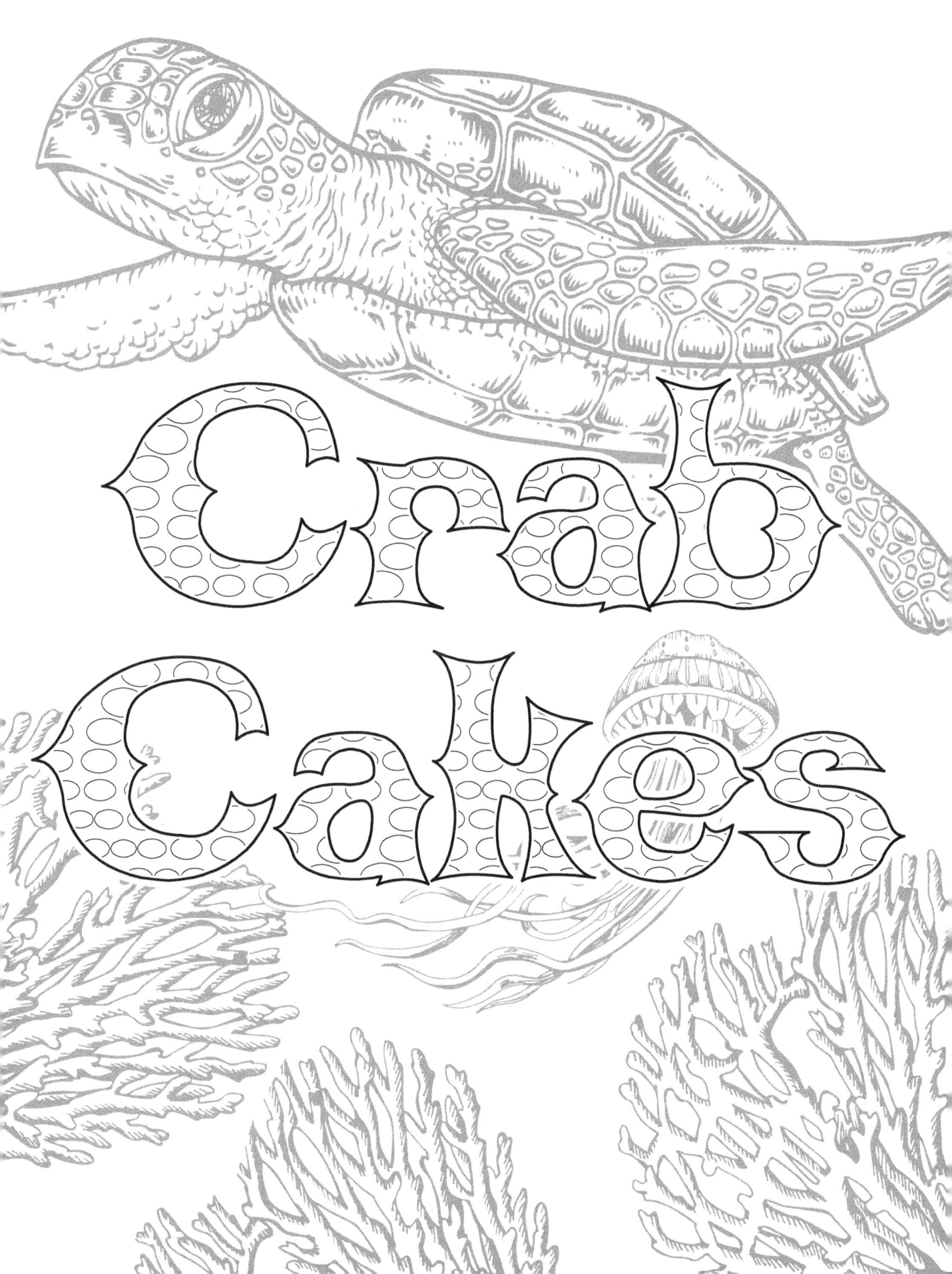

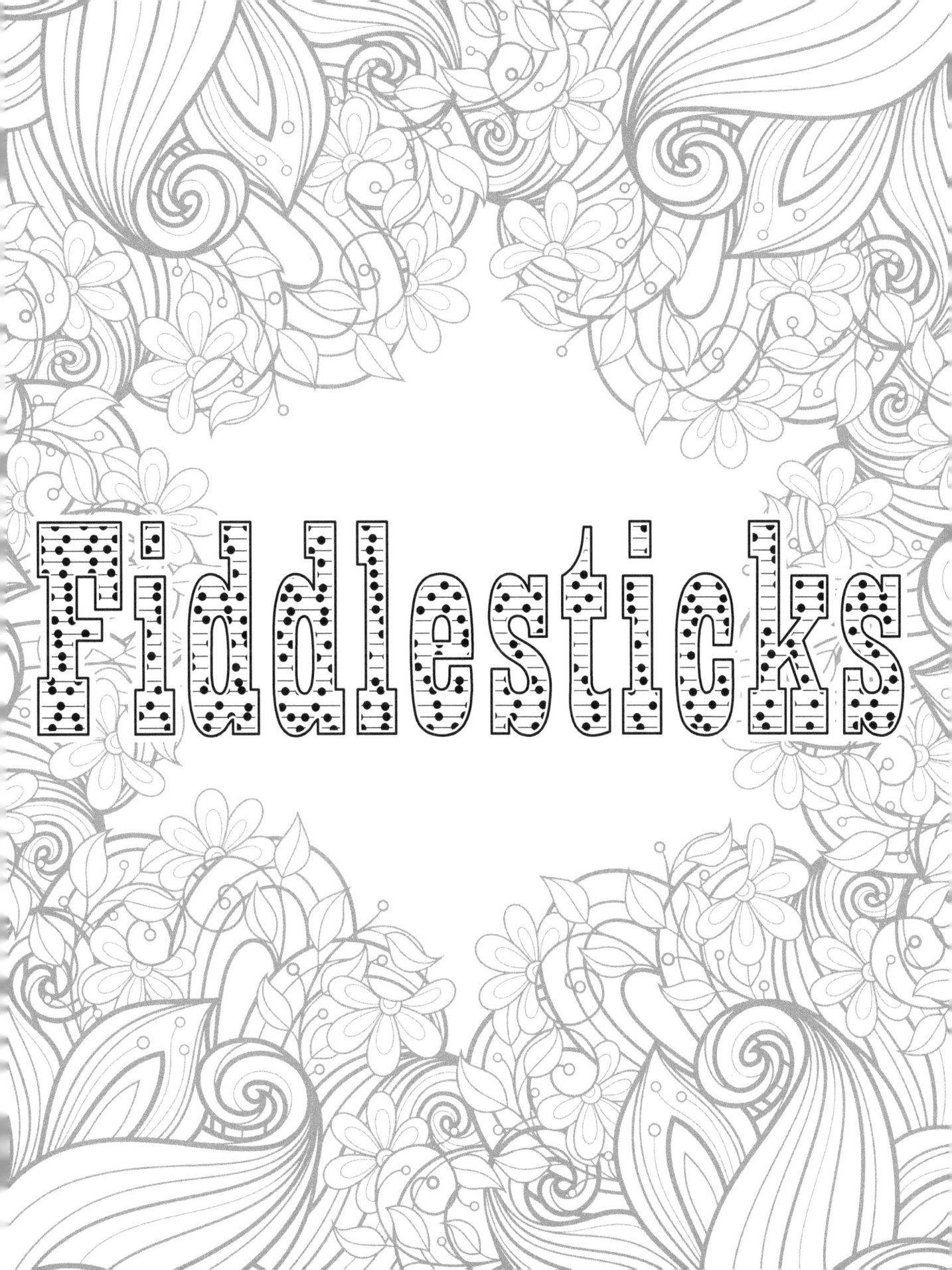

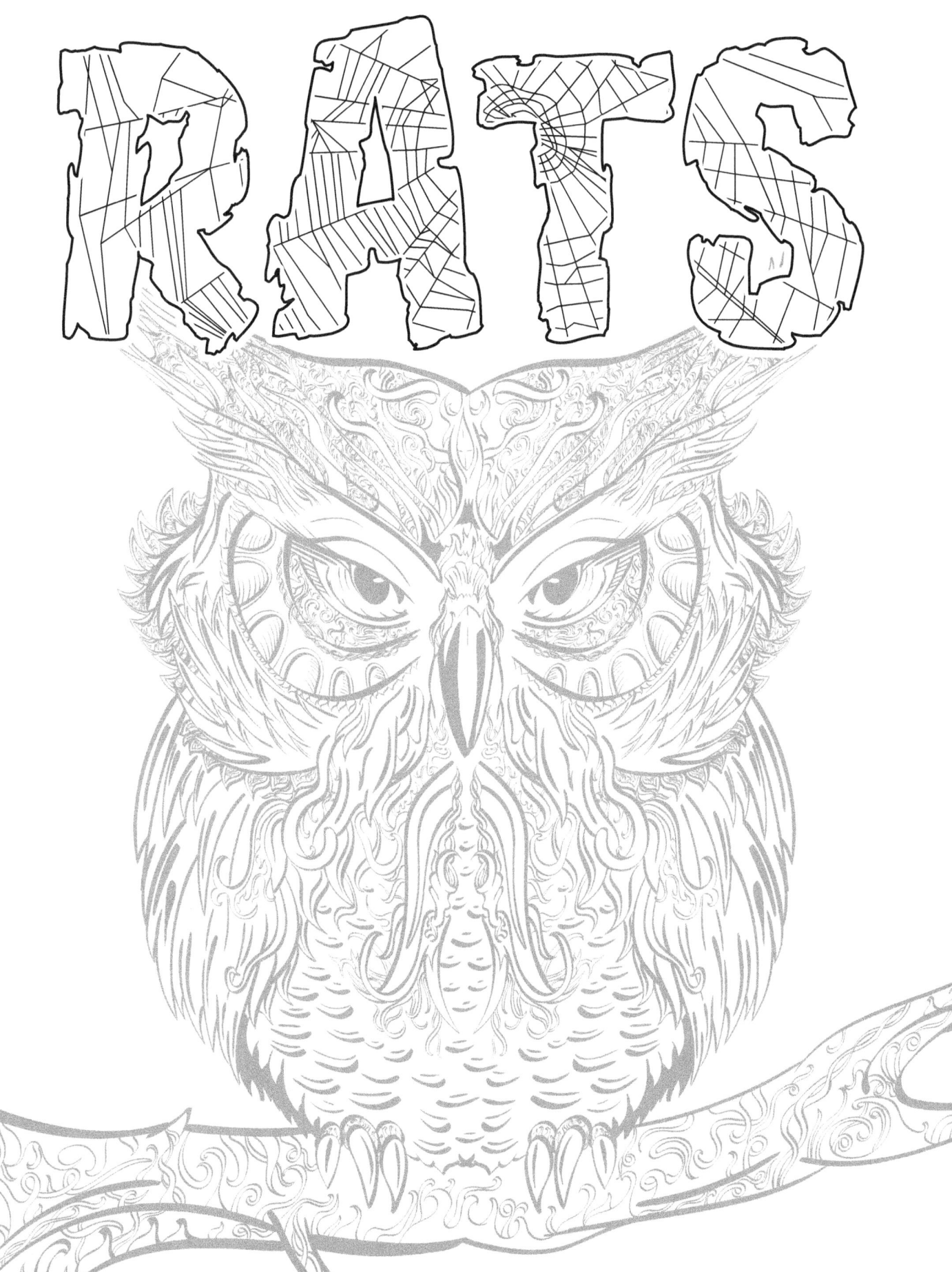

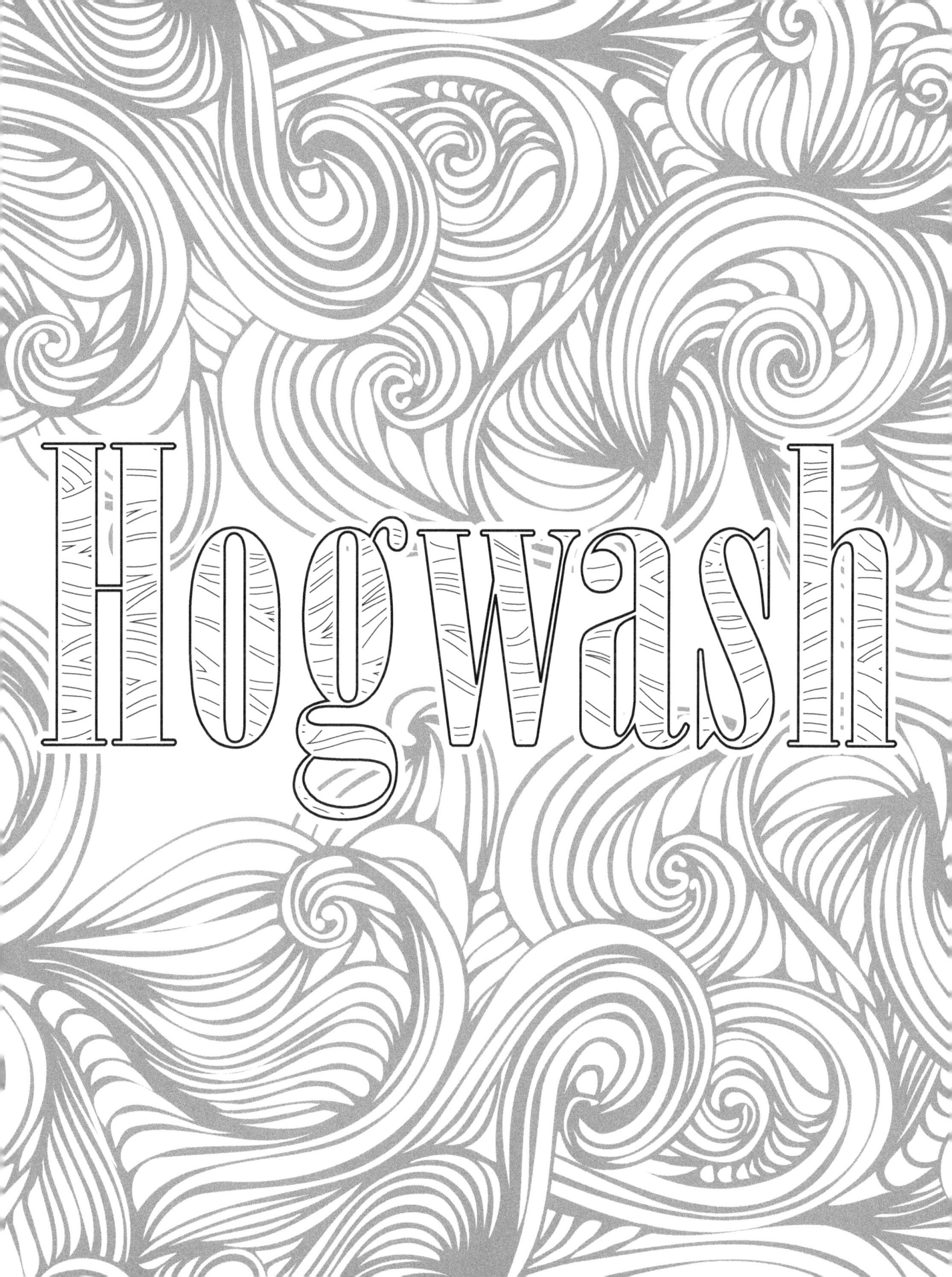

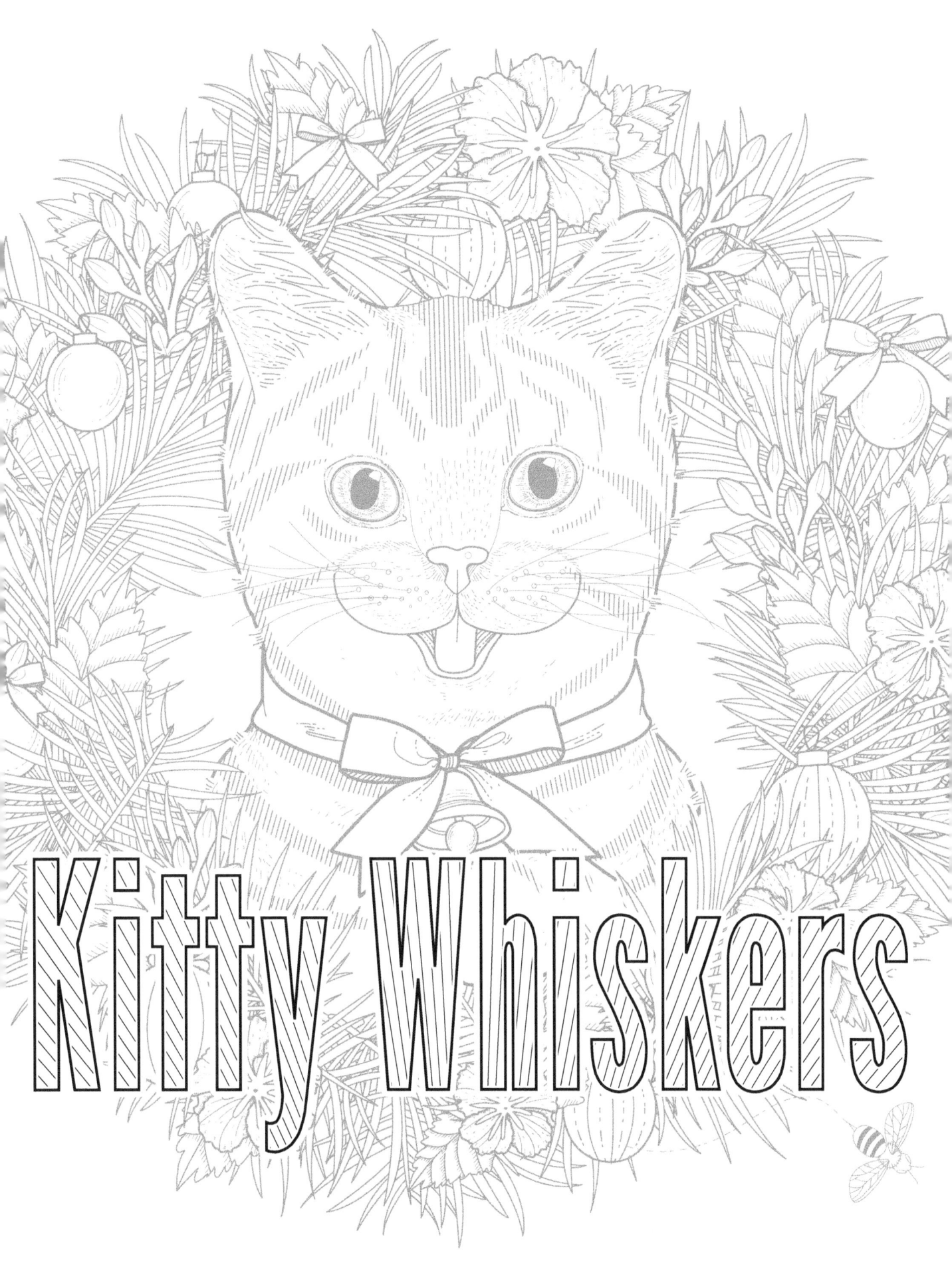

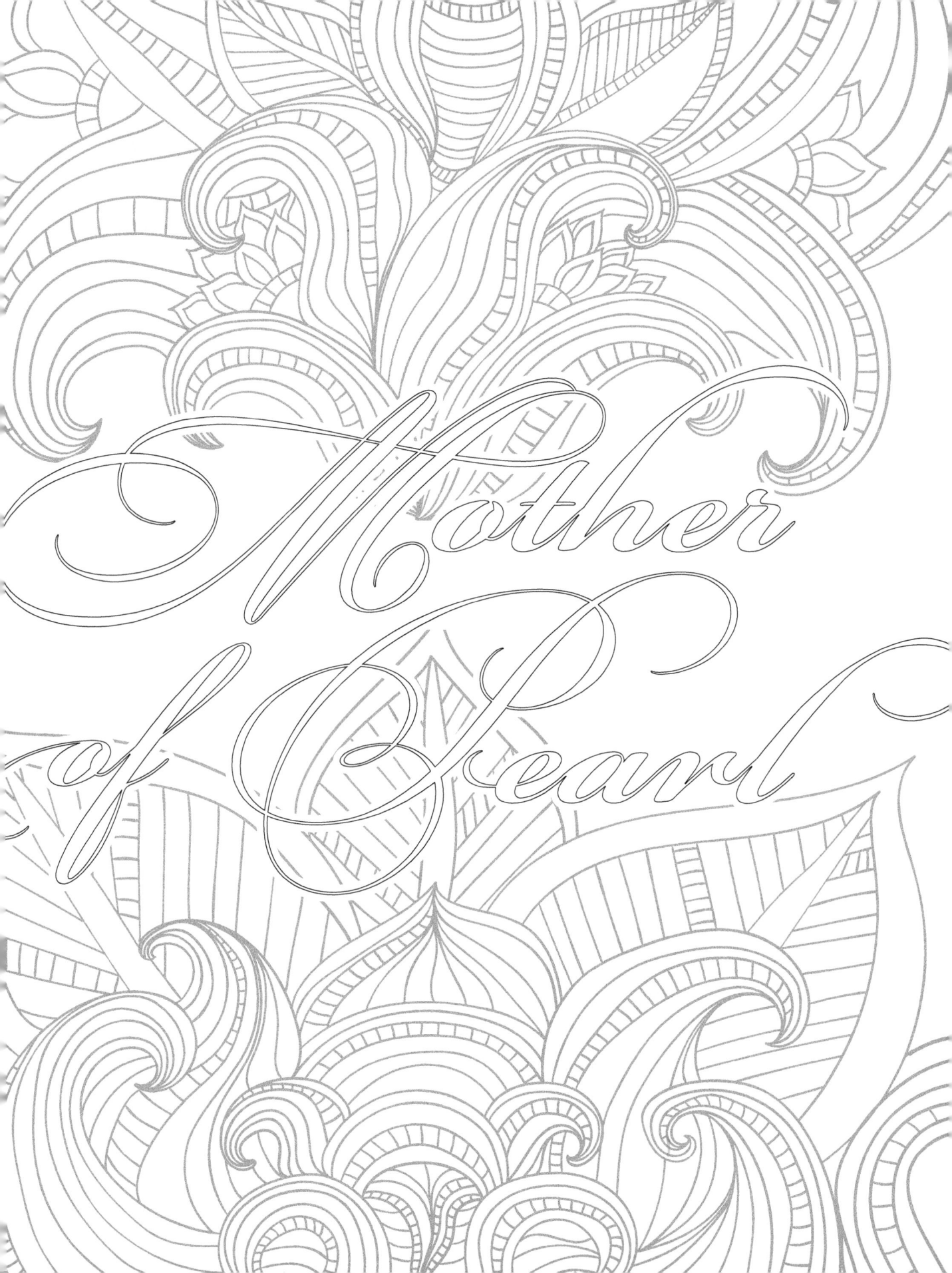

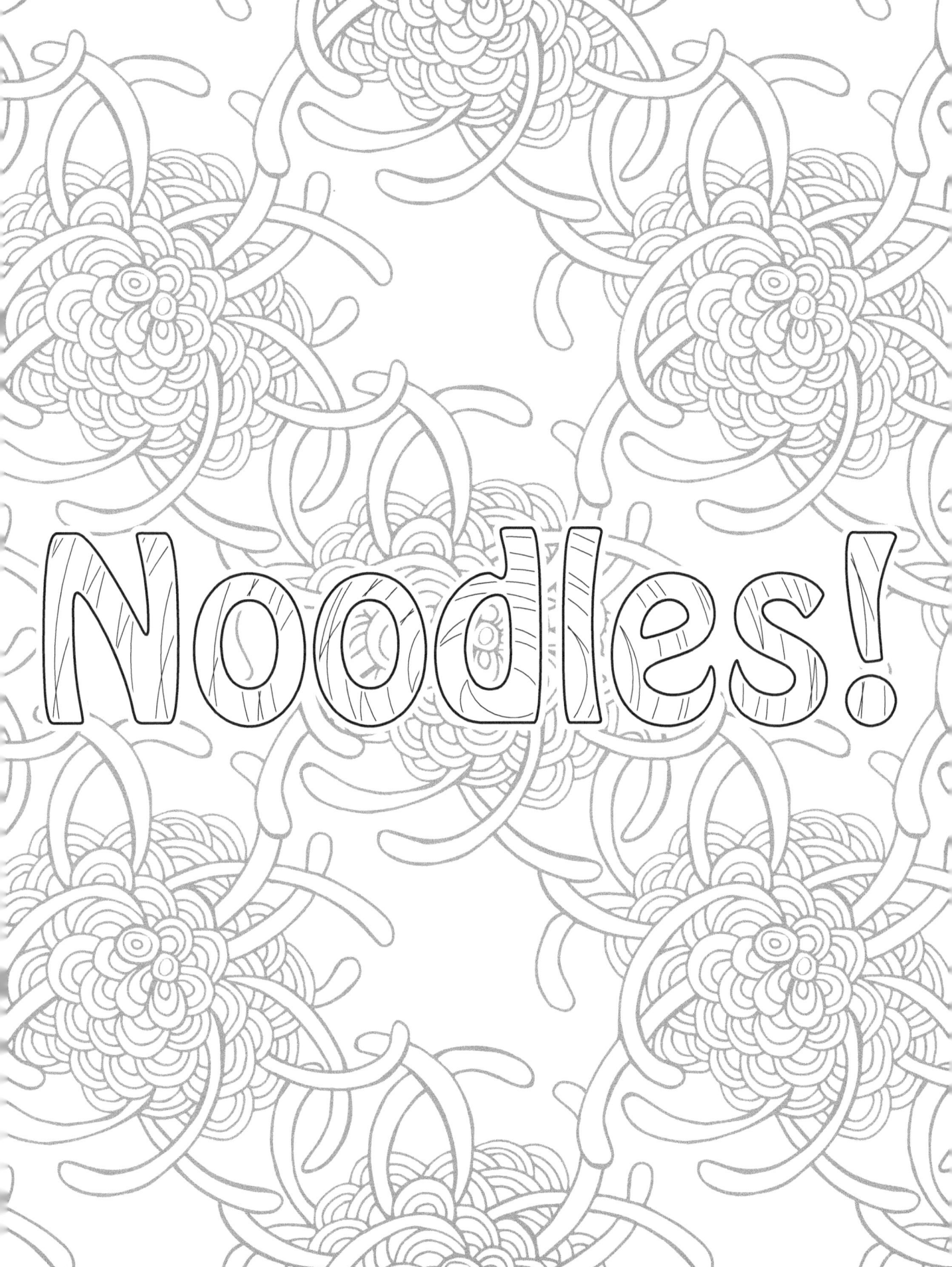

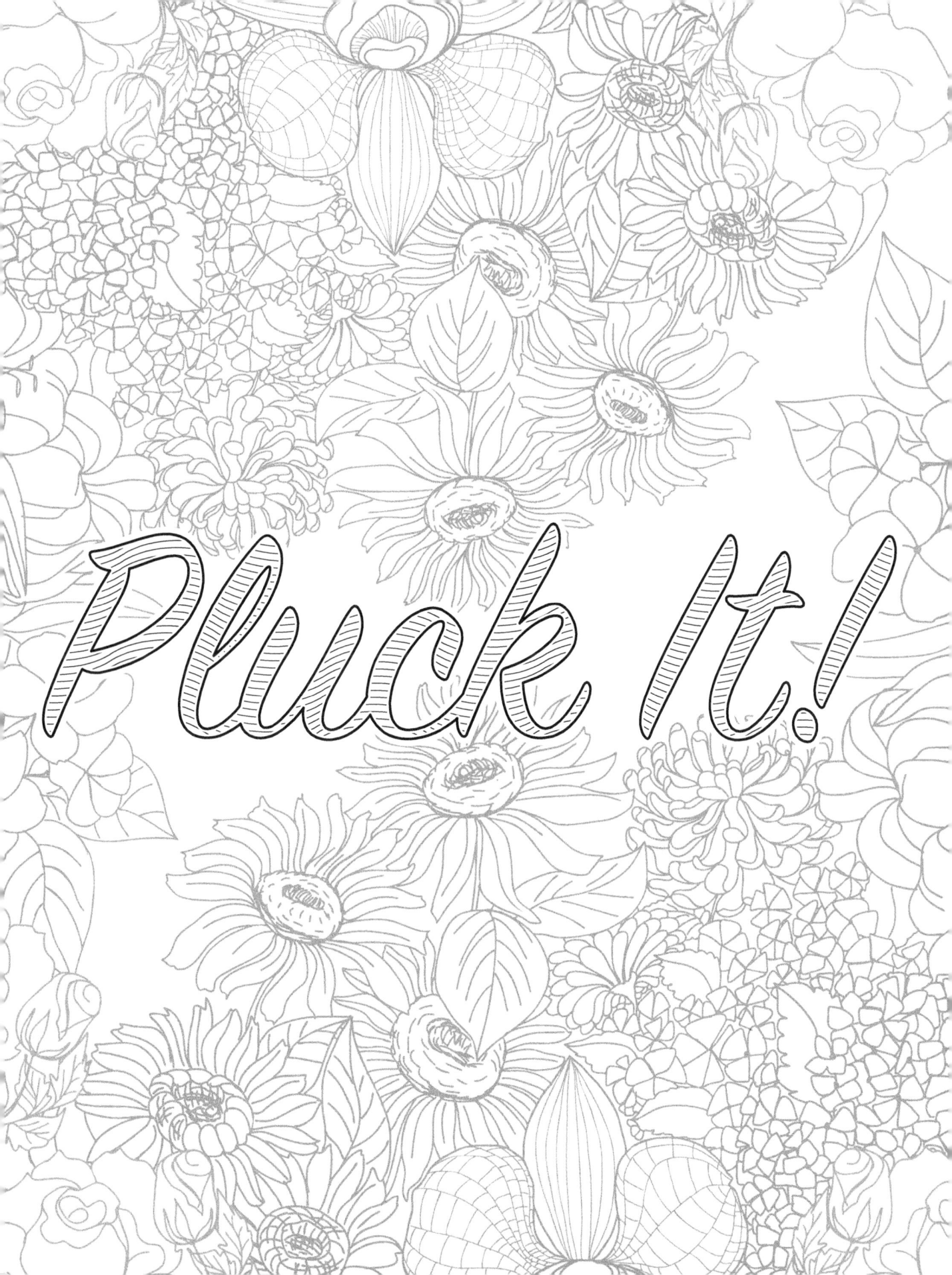

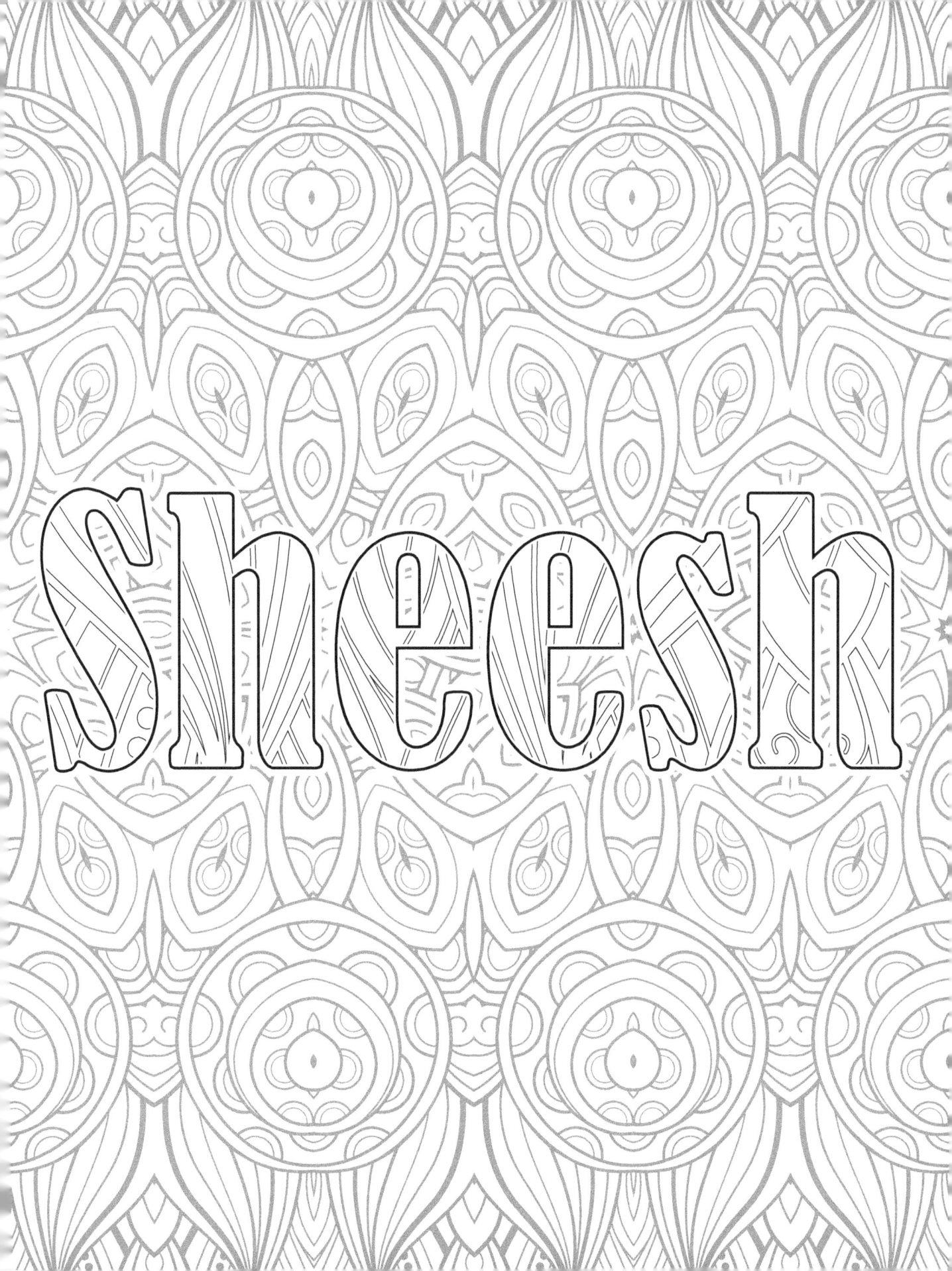

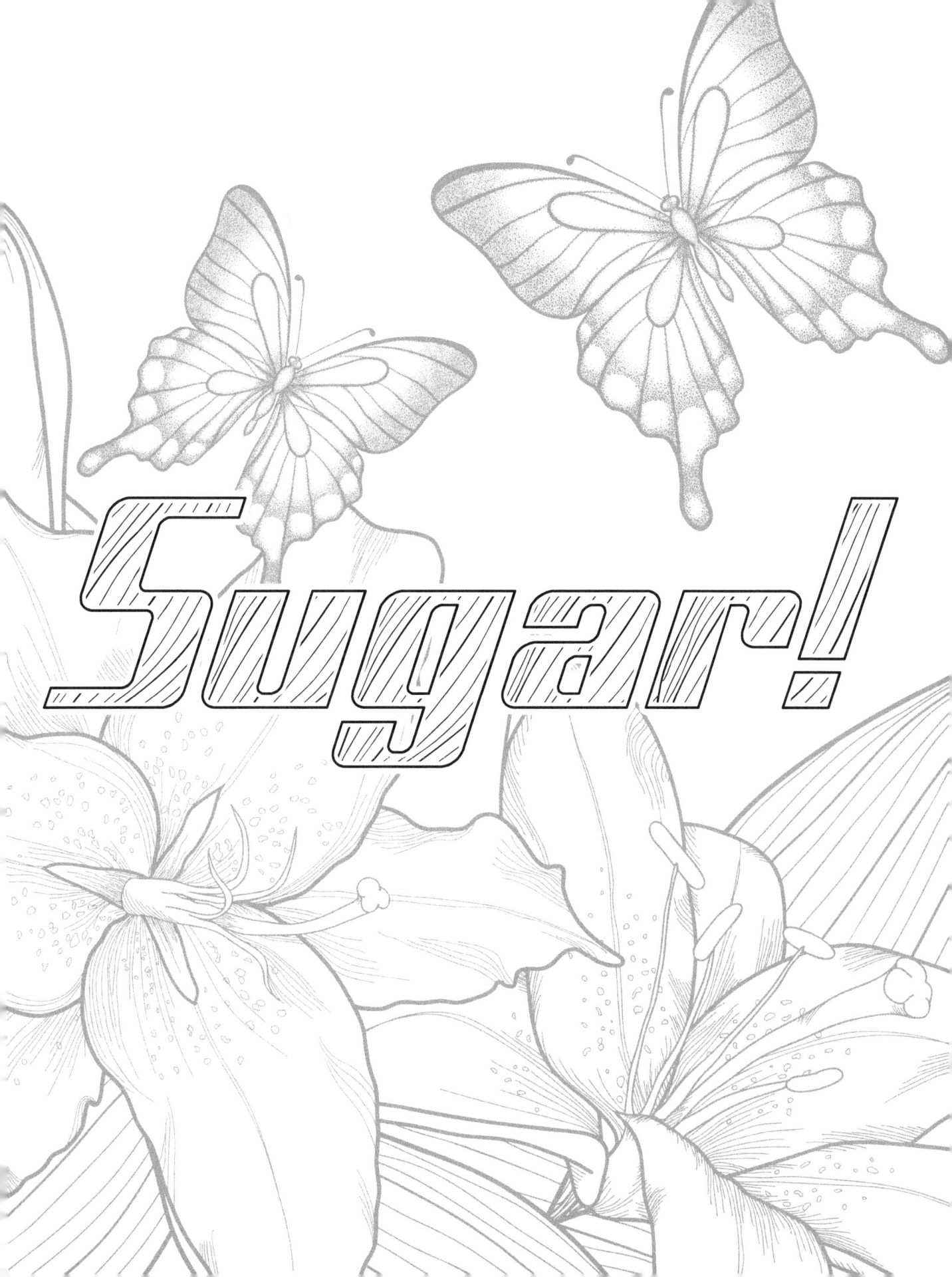

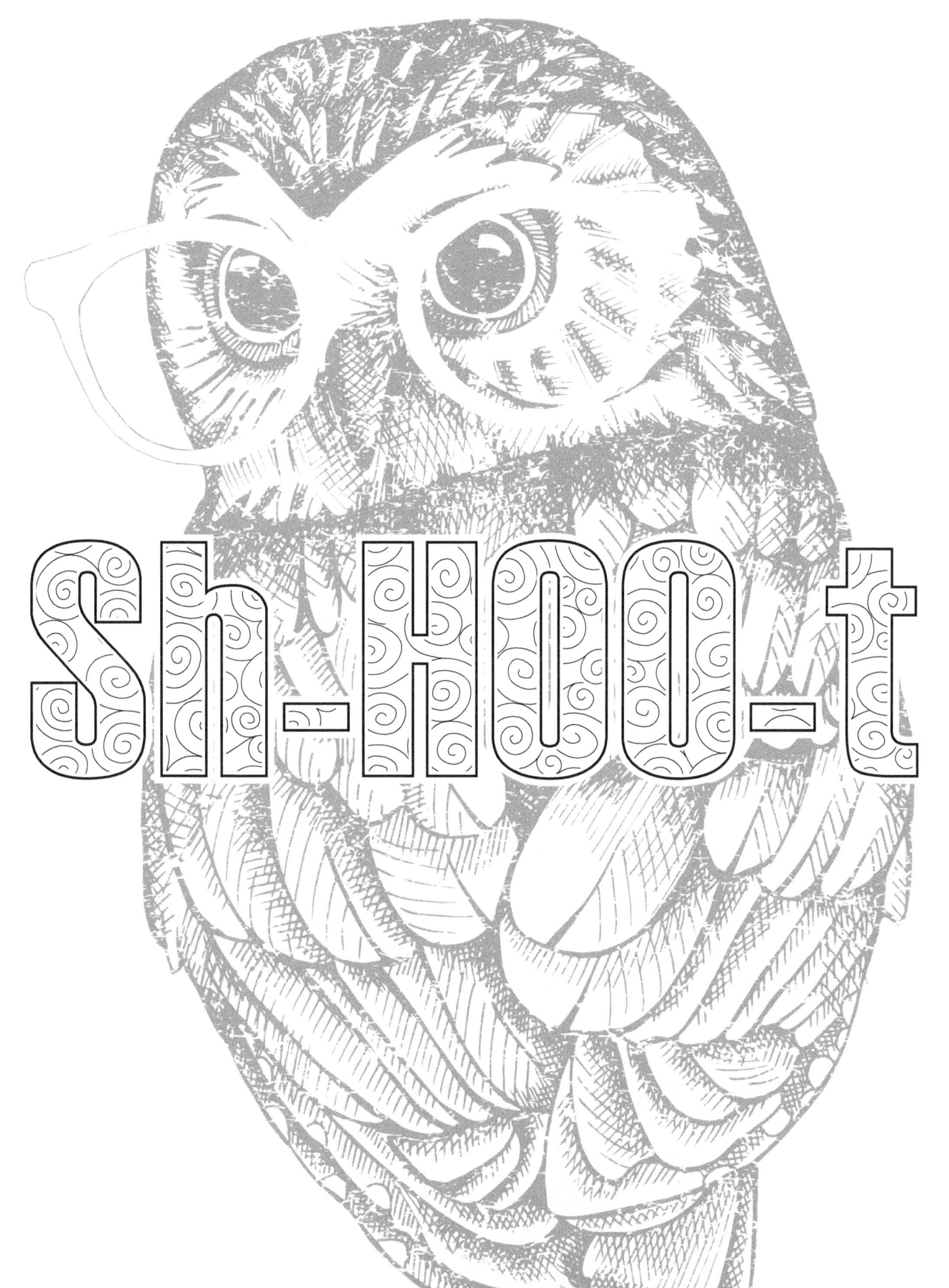

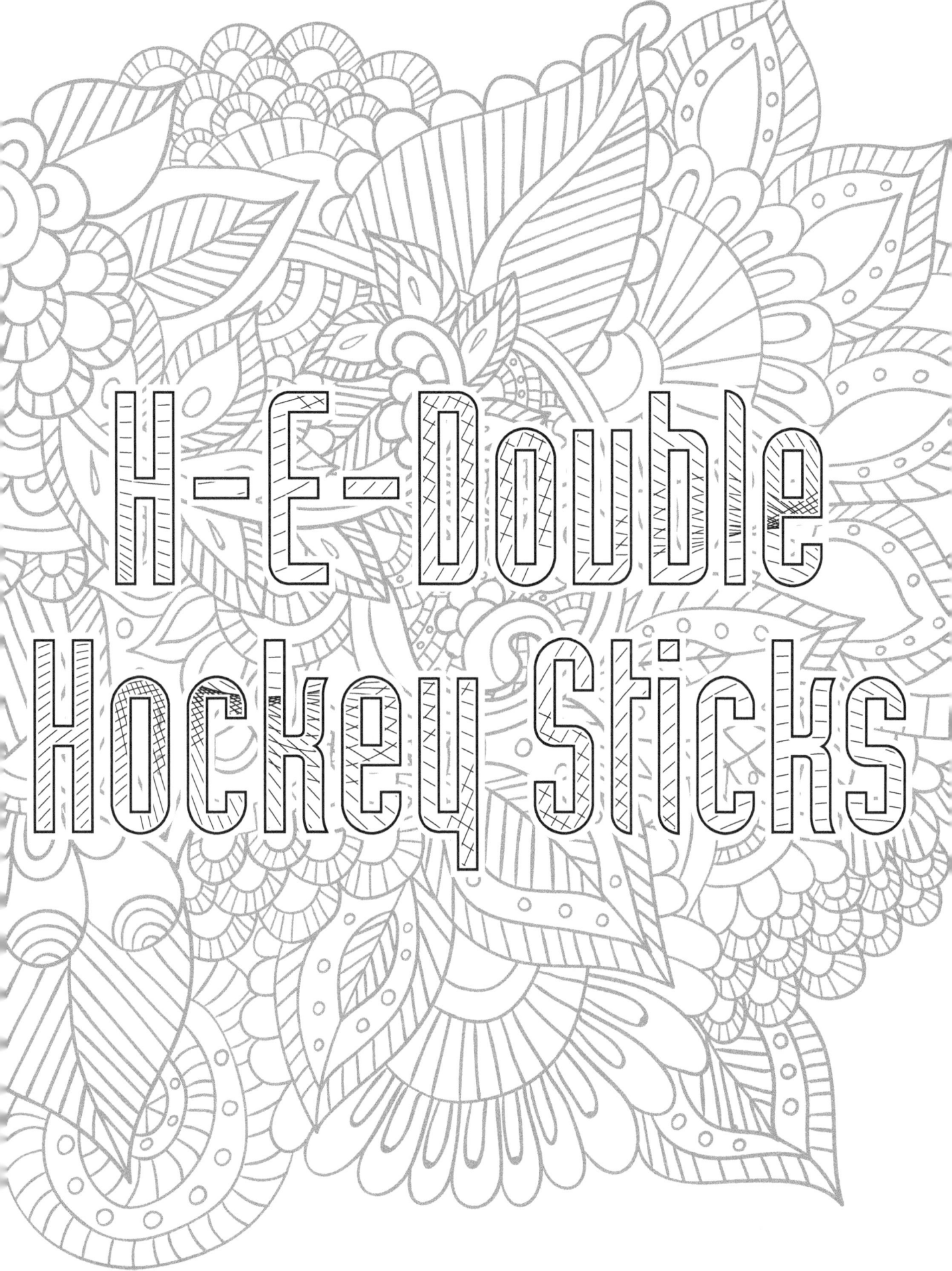

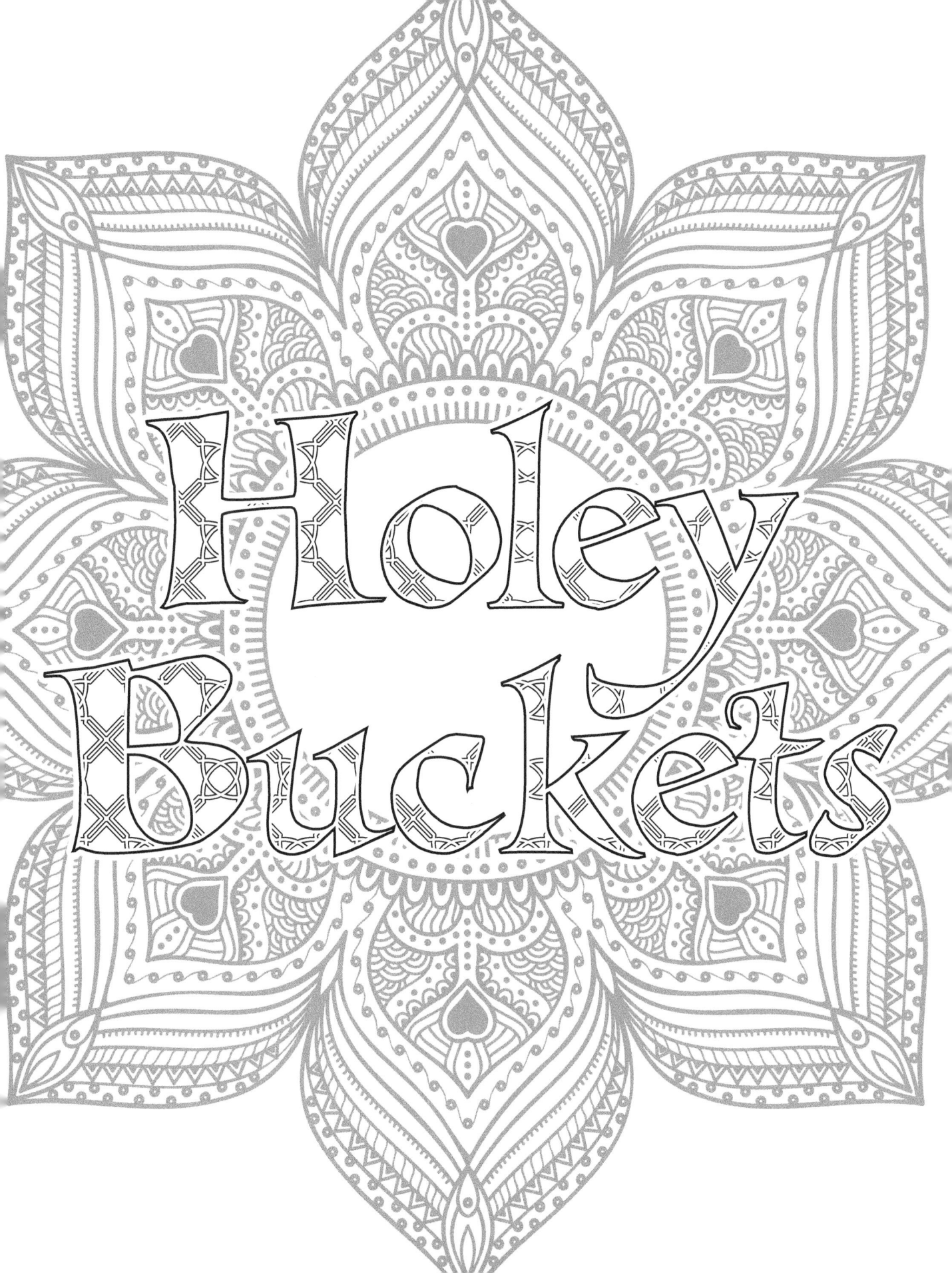

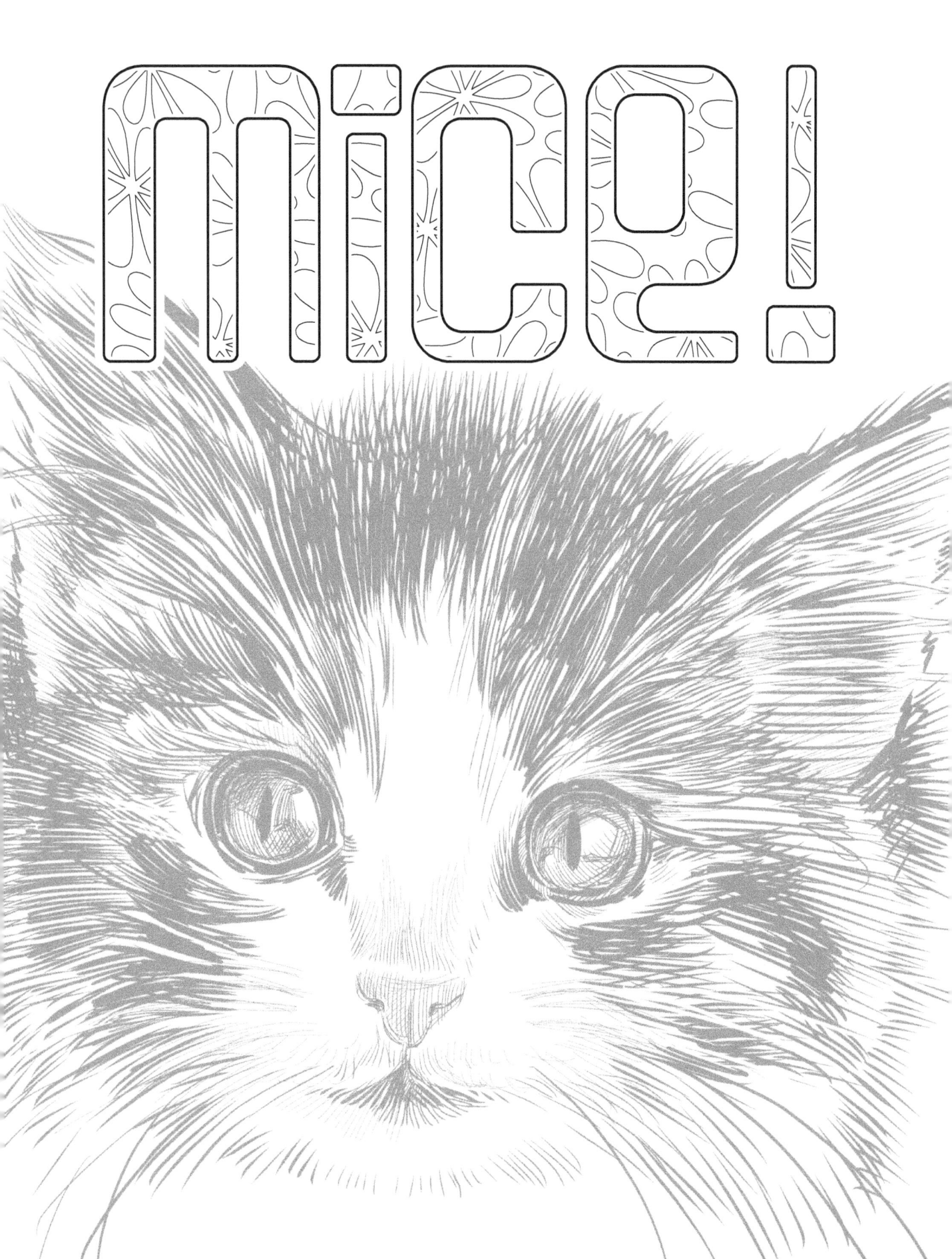

More books from Kingfisher Press:

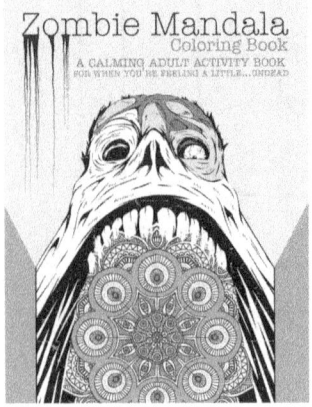

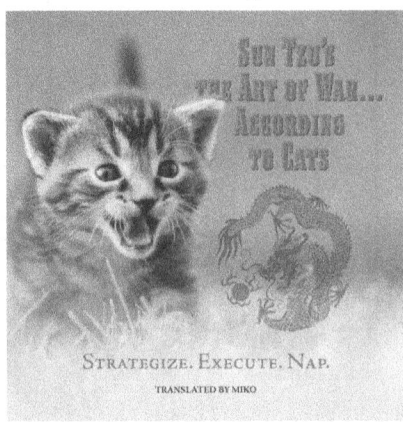

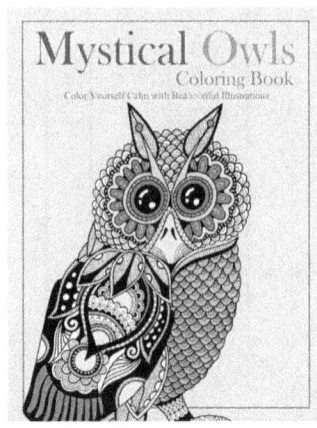

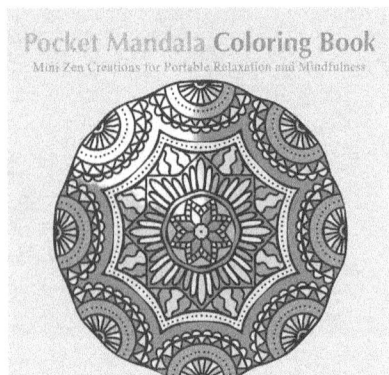

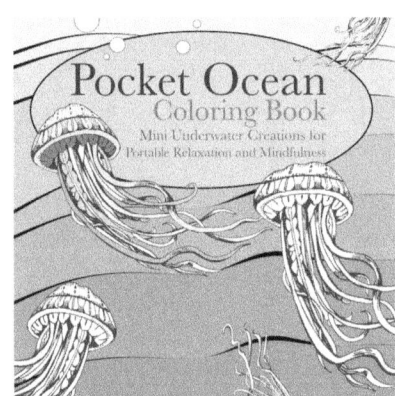

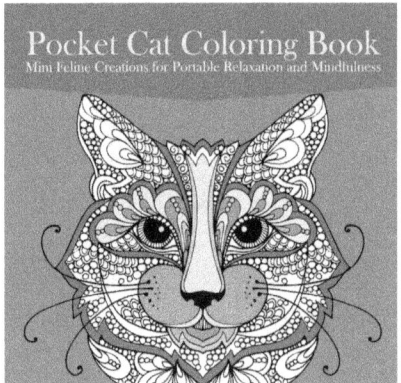

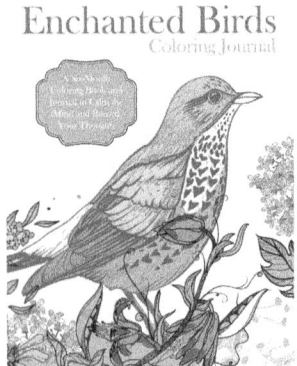

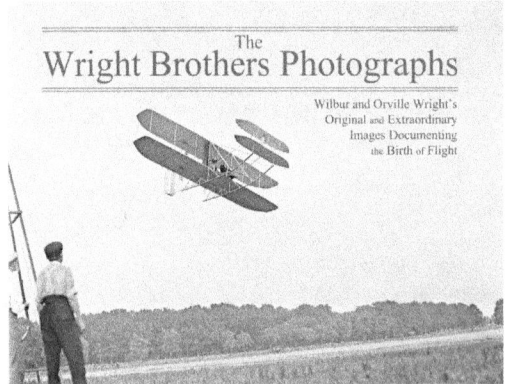

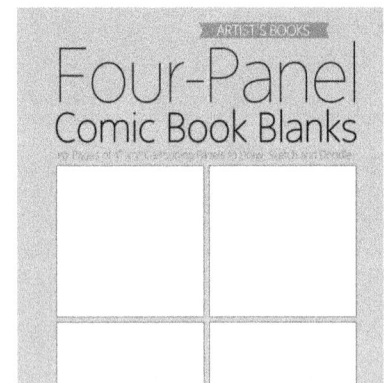

www.kingfisherpressbooks.com

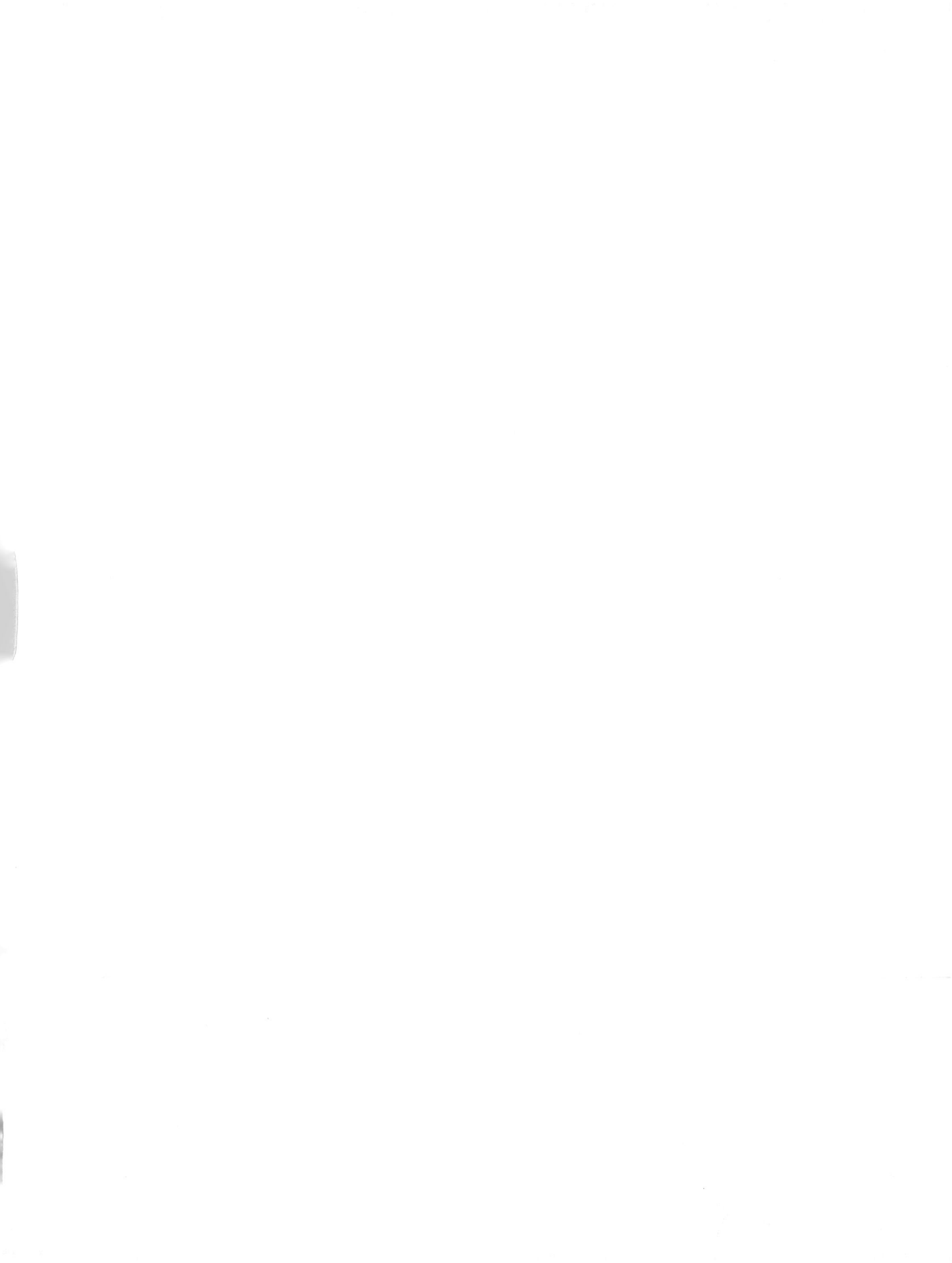

www.ingramcontent.com/pod-product-compliance
Lightning Source LLC
Chambersburg PA
CBHW080641190526
45169CB00009B/3455